# Reading Together

# The Wheels On The Bus

# Read it together

*The Wheels on the Bus*
is a humorous version
of the popular
nursery song with
illustrations showing
a group of young friends
having fun acting it out
in the garden.

Reading and singing this song aloud
is the best way to help your child get
to know and enjoy the book. Try to
choose a time that suits you both and
a place that's comfortable.

Now which one shall
I read this time?

The Wheels on
the Bus. That's my
favourite!

What is
he doing?

I think he's
making the
wipers work.

Talking together about
the story, rhyme and
pictures helps children
to make sense of the book.

Encourage your child to join in with you whenever they can. In this way they learn how the song goes and understand more about reading and books. A good way to do this is to let them finish the rhyme.

This version of the song invites children to join in with actions. It helps them remember the sequence of events and adds to their enjoyment.

Children's understanding of the book grows from talking about it. They might like to share their memories of bus rides or make up a story of what might happen on their next ride.

We hope you enjoy reading this book together.

First published 1998 by Walker Books Ltd
87 Vauxhall Walk, London SE11 5HJ

6 8 10 9 7 5

Illustrations © 1998 Andy Cooke
Introductory and concluding notes © 1998 CLPE/LB Southwark

Printed in Great Britain

ISBN 0-7445-4890-X

# The Wheels On The Bus

Illustrated by
## Andy Cooke

WALKER BOOKS
AND SUBSIDIARIES
LONDON • BOSTON • SYDNEY

The wheels on the bus go round and round,
Round and round, round and round.
The wheels on the bus go round and round,
All day long.

The bell on the bus goes ting-a-ling-ling!
Ting-a-ling-ling, ting-a-ling-ling!
The bell on the bus goes ting-a-ling-ling!
All day long.

The driver on the bus says, "Tickets, please!"
"Tickets, please!", "Tickets, please!"
The driver on the bus says, "Tickets, please!"
All day long.

The children on the bus bump up and down,
Up and down, up and down.
The children on the bus bump up and down,
All day long.

The wipers on the bus go swish, swish, swish!
Swish, swish, swish! Swish, swish, swish!
The wipers on the bus go swish, swish, swish!
All day long.

The baby on the bus goes,
"WAAHH, WAAHH, WAAHH!"
"WAAHH, WAAHH, WAAHH!"
"WAAHH, WAAHH, WAAHH!"
The baby on the bus goes,
"WAAHH, WAAHH, WAAHH!"
All day long.

The sister on the bus goes, "Ssh, ssh, ssh!"
"Ssh, ssh, ssh!", "Ssh, ssh, ssh!"
The sister on the bus goes, "Ssh, ssh, ssh!"
All day long.

The wheels on the bus go round and round,
Round and round, round and round.
The wheels on the bus go round and round,
All day long.

# Read it again

### Act it out
Like the children in the book, your child can use assorted boxes, chairs or cushions to act out the song with friends or teddies. They could design their own tickets, too.

### Sing it loud
Children can use home-made musical instruments to accompany the song. They can practise it to perform to you. You could even tape the event.

## New verses

You can sing the song together, making up some new verses.

## Map game

Together you could make a simple map of a bus route. Children could drive a toy bus along it, describing the journey as they go.

## I spy a bus ride

A bus ride is a good time to play "I Spy", looking around the bus and out of the window.

## Other versions

There are many versions of this popular song to look out for in libraries, supermarkets and bookshops. You can talk about the differences and, with some help, your child could make their own version.

# Reading Together

The *Reading Together* series is divided into four levels – starting with red, then on to yellow, blue and finally green. The six books in each level offer children varied experiences of reading. There are stories, poems, rhymes and songs, traditional tales and information books to choose from.

Accompanying the series is a Parents' Handbook, which looks at all the different ways children learn to read and explains how *your* help can really make a difference!

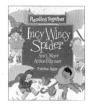   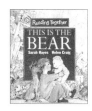  

     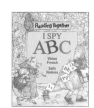

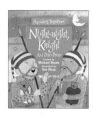